THE SOUND BOAT

WISCONSIN POETRY SERIES

Edited by Ronald Wallace and Sean Bishop

THE SOUND BOAT

NEW AND SELECTED POEMS

Judith Vollmer

The University of Wisconsin Press

Publication of this book has been made possible, in part, through support from the Anonymous Fund of the College of Letters and Science at the University of Wisconsin–Madison.

The University of Wisconsin Press
728 State Street, Suite 443
Madison, Wisconsin 53706
uwpress.wisc.edu

Gray's Inn House, 127 Clerkenwell Road
London EC1R 5DB, United Kingdom
eurospanbookstore.com

Printed in the United States of America
This book may be available in a digital edition.

Library of Congress Cataloging-in-Publication Data
Names: Vollmer, Judith, 1951– author.
Title: The sound boat : new and selected poems / Judith Vollmer. Other titles: Wisconsin poetry series.
Description: Madison, Wisconsin : The University of Wisconsin Press, [2022] | Series: Wisconsin poetry series
Identifiers: LCCN 2021041560 | ISBN 9780299336943 (paperback)
Subjects: LCGFT: Poetry.
Classification: LCC PS3572.O3957 S68 2022 | DDC 811/.54—dc23
LC record available at https://lccn.loc.gov/2021041560

for Ann and our families

and for

Mihaela Moscaliuc and Michael Waters

*I thought of how many places there are in the world that belong in this way to someone,
who has it in his blood beyond anyone else's understanding.*
—CESARE PAVESE, *THE DEVIL IN THE HILLS,*
1949, TRANSLATED BY R. W. FLINT

This is not hell, this is a street.
This is not death, this is a fruit stall.
—FEDERICO GARCIA LORCA, "OFFICE AND DENUNCIATION," *THE POET IN
NEW YORK*, TRANSLATED BY GALWAY KINNELL

If you take the moon in your hands
and turn it round
(heavy, slightly tarnished platter)
you're there
—H.D., "A DEAD PRIESTESS SPEAKS," *UNCOLLECTED
AND UNPUBLISHED POEMS*

Contents

from *Reactor* (2004)

from *The Door Open to the Fire* (1997)

from *Level Green* (1990)

THE SOUND BOAT

Roadside Tavern

The front stoop frost-sketched,

welcoming twilight spirits.

Bikers and docs off work line the bar,

a frieze of repair and solace.

I slide my backpack down

onto Earth's spinning cask.

The floor lifts, displays its seams

and shines with the two or three

colors—ochre or russet,

sienna or slag—

the bottom mud of our rivers

once yielded for bricks.

Young Jane Jacobs

—Scranton, 1925

Every August other children whisper
Tonight all the lakes turn upside down—

I know that, but no one knows
I am a bird, not a girl, so lifting off

eighty feet up, I see rock veins cross
under the Lackawanna, people

sleeping in coke ovens.
School bores me. I am not

pretty or handsome, and startle
with my beak nose, but

I read trowel lines on cement,
footsteps going to buy milk.

I count stripes on awnings, bars on grates,
women stuffing breads into sacks. Peer inside

chimneys and tall windows,
take a cold-metal drink from the yard hose,

save some for the storm-cellar doors
sagging like tongues. Now my city

is my web. Come September,
when the bell rings

I will be late again,
sit on the edge of my bed, one shoe on,

head in hand. *I'm thinking,*
figuring something out.

Doppelgänger

—old Peoples Savings Bank on Pittsburgh's former "Wall Street"

Tower of verdigris and terra cotta rosettes,
temple of vaults and glass walls
trembling, fractured,
you've stitched yourself

onto me, second spine
or mind, shadow and
conductor, my walk interrupted
by your twenty-seven
convex windows moon-silvered

so I'm spangled, tilted.
Lounging genius, once
you threaded the war money
of the city fathers

up your spiral stair
counting, hiding
sons of the rich
from The Ardennes to Kandahar.
Now your bronze doors

won't open
while you refashion,
tongue new money
through your neo-

Romanesque arches
damp with blankets and piss.

A Visit from Milosz

Expecting a rich man's face? I was born with these eyebrows,

they filter my over-thinking and ferment my tears. I did not come from legacy filth.

Did you forget you also stink of worsted wool? Don't be like me—*laskawa melancholia*

—they say I have it. Scatter your dark thoughts

and embrace Literature. Un-sequin the sky cocktail,

count the constellations that way, your own way.

Of course I sense I feel guilt

over leaving Nature, but I say you can't interrupt your own life.

Once I carried the scent of the Atlantic, musk salt on my fingertips.

Why Berkeley? I had to leave the war zones, but I took Poland with me.

My Vistula, my Sacramento, with those two rivers

one life is more than possibly three.

Pittsburgh Maps

Speck Street

Their old well became the latrine that fed
the garden's sweet harvest eaten by starlings,
humans, dogs, mice. All traces of the house
gone, no print visible on the dusty grass.
Street named for the pigs of Pig Alley, pushed
downhill to slaughter for bacon with potatoes
and fresh payday eggs.

West End Overlook

All three rivers telescope away,
the basin foggy, gray. First Imperial War
on U.S. soil, gateway to the West after
the demolition of Iroquois Nation. Drive
or walk up through Beltzhoover to get here:
killer cop, synagogue shooter, killer cop—
all three raised a few streets over. Scratched
lovers' codes on the balustrade. Maple,
ash, locust, cherry, hawthorn drape
the hillside, fog lifts and the rivers lens back
in my direction. Behind me the white
militia screens are up late talking to
the white soldiers in the long civil cold war.

Carnegie Library

When I first learned August Wilson left school
after false accusation of plagiarism I walked up
the steps to visit where he taught himself
and became a writer. My throat crashed,
tears fell and locked. Ghost-scars
and words, ballads, rails ran wild along the tables.

The Seven Hills

Flagstaff, Troy, Mount Washington, West End—
please, if you're far, teach me your way to Seven.
Your Aleppo, your Prague and Rome pulse
and whisper here. I finish slightly East,
beyond the Atom Smasher and the Electric
Valley to Roundtop I, II, and III.

Roundtop I, II, and III

Seen from the air the domes
align imperfectly, curved;
did they show the way to the great
gatherings and summer fishing
at the rivers, and the way home
into shelter of the small ridges?

Unnamed

The shrine to Whiskey Witch tilts
above Turtle Creek. She painted
her eyes acetylene blue then hopped
a train West, dragging her broken
boots, grocery cart, and ancient
grandchild and dog.

Young George Harrison

Meticulous, he made all his solos
different, sound-sculpting them into the tone cabinets,
testing frequencies, splitting
    rotations, ear to glass and wood,
        compression and crossover,
thus all his leads would fit the songs.

He bought the Gretsch because of Atkins,
and after a slide solo he owed to Elmore James
the cabinets juddered and shook
        beside the Maestro Fuzztone's
harsh, distorted, divine overdrive.   All that

came years after the daily bus,
head pressed against the window-
frame conducting: listen to tires
crush cinders and satin the rail tracks.
    Who knows you get sweet burnt-wail
    out of the Delta? Who knows what off the sea—
    bird curtains and moon milk.
    Keening he lost in Ireland.
Hider, sure he was behind the hedges,
smoking, blotting out ladies'
teeth clacking, purses snapping,
here a small bird cracks a twig
    and a wire basket scrapes a door ten meters back.
    Listen for sounds no one hears.

Mother brings him tea all night,
he works till he drifts,
sees sand that made the glass. Green-gray surf.
    He pretends it's hot glass on a cool table.
    Liverpool sets the table and he's ready to serve.

The Diagonals

This side of the city the train
divides the river from its slopes;
on the other, jackhammers butt up

against hills and call back. When I
was young before my brain
fully fused, say twenty-four or so, I drove
around at night playing which

streets run completely East or West,
North/South, but most run South/
Southwest or North/Northwest, plus

crooked, and/or disconnected, up to
Canada or down into the Bluegrass.
From my bus aisle seat facing front,
I feel I'm not myself and not

both of me; could be the election
or the chemo, brain and gut equally
knotted. Heavy hills lean down

and their hedges encrusted
with road salt eat train-wail, mix it
into wind twisting rough branches,
that keening sound my parents

coming down from the Great Lakes riding
the long train looking for home. Still here
but I lose my sense of direction

in the diagonals weirdly praying, which
I've only ever thought of as sitting, quiet,
the train must be halfway to Harrisburg by now
or gone Northwest to Green Bay

inside a sound-tunnel maybe mimicking spiral-
waves from Space said to be gelatinous
or glutinous, less like fusilli, more

like linguini, to give myself a picture.
Threading my way through
unknown black holes I'm blinded
by hydrogen walls and fire bubbles

and my own eyes that register
then color the sounds, or at least
attach the color, blinded by
the indetectable solar wind.

Angel Dust Elegy

Reefer, check. Baggie of Quaaludes,
check; pool of blue Viagra

and the campus cop complained:
"You boys ought to be whipped

if you need that." We girls
had splayed ourselves

along the couch in our black tanks
and white boxers and were slowly

passing out. Languid, we called ourselves
odalisques, then our dean,

who lied for us, drove us
to the clinic and waited

to sign us out. He who played
air guitar behind his office door,

ex-Navy Seal lived with his aunt
until her death. Francophile,

acquisition sleuth of Gustons
and Averys for his beloved

neighborhood museum down past
a lonely street of bronze stars

and sulfur torches
years before I never took powder

up my nose, restrained by his kindness
and closeted patriarchal wing.

Street Fair

—for Ann

I'm smearing myself with lemon-balm against the stinging gnats, humming to the San Marzanos you planted and secured onto their tall poles. Speed-weeding, friends due in ten, I catch the familiar smell: sewer gas, city trying to patch a century's fracturing. I stash my trowel, hose the walk to fresh metallic tang. I'm hiding behind the hedge, love, calm, now, as we were reckless, then, driving fast, out dancing ten to close, breakfast at three, home to bed, our starship. Young girls are stepping off the 67F, in from the country, gleaming unguents and silver hoops, their precision-cutoffs and crisp tops slice the humidity. One wears a flower crown, another a dozen copper bracelets—arrivals—fryers sizzle, klezmer wails, smoke stretches into dusk you murmur into: "Sometimes late July still makes me sad." Me too, we should shut the country down, paid up, through August. I say it every year, clear the quasi-collective head. Beloved dead, swelling into wider circles, will you know us on arrival, hurtling downhill no brakes? No camping no fires in Frick's park. Dear Night, dim the house lights, sugar the bricks, the street opening onto our new long dance.

Ovarian

—*after* Maman, *among the spider sculptures of Louise Bourgeois*

My t-shirt celebration began

under April's limoncello sun,

street hushed, my porch-sit concentration

zoomed in on the wolf spider

carrying babies on her back,

a carpet-ride vibration along the straightaway

top step. Soon she was busy under the kitchen sink

feeding droplets of milk to her hatchlings.

Mother, show me

the tapestry pouch you stitched for me.

I'll implant it in my stripped and scoured

belly, now that I'm down to the joists

and studs, old womb tossed

into the surgeon's bin;

the pouch will dissolve, too,

silk of my silk,

see where it flies, our new nest

or bird roost. Or count any numbers or flights

our old ages add up to.

Eyes are watching me—

one casts a strand onto the table,

onto grapes in the glass bowl—

Does everything   Does anything

see me, bald and wiry, hauling myself

down and up the porch steps?

Were ovaries my second set of eyes?

I thought so, after the eighty-hour work weeks

when the lead sinkers

said *Take a break, we're getting a little blurry.*

Were they

turgid capsules of grief I had to release?

Don't look back

the kind doctor said.

If eyes, what if I stepped

inside them before they left the bin for good?

Say I was sitting on LB's eyeball bench

under *Maman's* steely eye

after my parents and my four friends died

and I held onto them

too tightly. Don't review.

Under my long skirt I saw

linen hem   sandal straps   marble-

mirror of the plaza,

rooms beneath, new rooms

I'm scavenging for doors, window frames,

panes of glass, steel mesh.   You could call it

joining the orb weavers, the scaffold weavers, or

reading, climbing   I tighten and strengthen

putting my full weight   leg by leg

pulling on my two good lungs

lifting or threading my way back into the house,

sticky palms and coated tongue

starting with the light-

mote that slid onto my cheek

two weeks past Equinox.

The Reader

Her voice
like a conductor motioned me
forward, close, up to the front,
the black slate's letters were crisp

streaming their high music in through my
eyeglass-less eyes. Don't be afraid of the blurring
or the flares, they can fix that, she said, leading
me into the Green Circle beside her desk,
three or four chairs

for slow readers. I saw *sparrow*
or *suggest*, thought *surgery* and how would I
live without my eyes they would pluck
leaving only spiders flashing, blinking,
my eyeballs sliced midway like corks, and

dipped in chalk dust.   Her surprise
as I bent my head into the book which
had an inside and an outside,
sheets of rain sealing the margins,

she came to me and opened another book
and another of large letters and smaller ones.
I was braided, finally, onto pages, filling,
and I saw how tall she was,

my conductor, a white pine   all her needles
threading more music into me

till I laughed when she read "germ of sadness"
and I heard "wheat germ" doing its crunching,
it was April and nearly
my first full year of school
had passed without reading. I heard her

click the fluorescents off—Look children, we have plenty
of light, she said, Look at your fingernails and your neighbor's
teeth. Spring light! she said, and it was very old, newly
arriving from the long Universe brushing us,
here in our Northern Hemisphere.

The Sound Boat

1.

I left the new street for the old,

cats fed, kitchen scrubbed, workbench

cleared for the deep blue bolt I unroll nightly

between stacks that reach the roof.

I smooth the dark blue, chalk the regions. Last summer I cut

Northern mountains from serge, lined crevasses with raw

silk. I gauged snowfalls over a half-century, then fastened

the peaks' white caps. I stayed in the mountains

five months, took their air into my lungs

mornings along the river that rushed down-mountain

fast as bird-flight. Staring up at the fourteeners

I stitched granite bands from bark and twine.

My night windows gaze down at me while I work by lamp.

By day I repair.

Elbow and knee patches, gown and skirt hems,

work-pants I seal with canvas. Sometimes a child's soft leather shoe.

All else briefly celebratory: bride or broker,

widow or groom caught in my measure.

Colors, hefts they don't know they love, or know but have never possessed.

Frothed with beads and lace, champagne and coin, a bride once

threw herself into a grave three months after. Her name sits along the river.

I moved South, laid shreds of gauze for wind, twill for dunes, frayed batiste

for surf. I secured the coast with button shards and I bolstered a thinning reef.

I swam beside the firewater fish: see the dayglo strands I used for eyes and scales.

I followed those strange creatures, they ate well, so did I! Dear friend,

show me how to lie down in the Everglades and look beneath:

I will satin-stitch a cache of seed pearls for your hair.

The way West: straightaway and canyon. Jan mapped it:

cinder powder and steel-filings pin her steady route.

Start in *Diondega*: place of ancients: the before-Pittsburgh/blood of others/blood of ours.

2.

Tonight I roll up my cloth and lift a glass to crazy-genius Archimedes:

How many grains to fill the universe, dear Sand Reckoner? How do

your levers and spirals work? I hammered silver into a mirror

and you struck fire at the masts of your enemies' ships: Sand Reckoner's

city, defended. I study my glass and refill, ignorant

of war, sick of home front. What can a mender do but mend.

3.

There is only one I love as much as the one I love.

I have missed you like a child

unaware of how sad her face looks.

Old city, I've come East for your long day and endless night:

down in the street, between the turtle fountain and the iron head

the party shouts and sings, sweats and snakes, swells into a throb

or momentum of sound. Dancers circle

an umbrella pine necklaced by a wire fence,

the day-star shoots its final, sharp rays,

windows flash and a ray delivers

onto my balcony railing a long slim

bar of acid-yellow fire, a candle, hissing,

pulling light up through something,

a sort of boat of sound,

maybe, workers yell into phones,

thread through the party to get home, kids

rustle, laughing, shoppers'

bags snap, sunset

simmers itself, slightly, a caprice,

before it slides down through then behind the tall

apartments whose windows blink on.

The sound boat eats till it swells

red on green, purple on cobalt,

dancers breathing, feeding—

last light kisses the sound,

the crowd and jubilation lift themselves up—

I want to step off and onto

the boat—gaseous tangerine chiffons

hovering, all the figures in the street

backlit with full-body halos

drift upward onto the sound boat—

The loudest red orange yellow waves

slow my needles and replace

them with magenta, then darkest blue, a cooling place.

The Immolation

I don't know what I'm looking at driving pulling over afraid in the storm   I see high up across
the river a steaming thing spitting siding and roof—Burst—fire hisses onto the porch that
hangs like a jaw, cliff pulling at it, falling deeper into mudslide, third this spring—the spring
after three winters: iced-March April front of May   Now I see a tree? lurch, strike metal—A
boy? sledge-hammering a stripped-down car   Lightning is aging him and oxidizing the house
but he—no fear—keeps smashing headlights windshield   soaking hair storm-whipped boy a
broken/breaking steel tree what is this world why worthy of him up there his own house dying
his one and only   my feeble benediction, that the house not fall, that trees lit up like x-rays
might show us a way   their fine intelligence bending down to the river.

Little Body

Even here, capsuled and tubed
I am riding Earth's body-blender, trees
sipping rushing water and natural lethal uranium, I too
am filtering through my belly the benzene and Mon River water
threading hospital pipes while bile and phlegm
keep spilling from my body which is
healing up. I'm celebrating my body my tremor vessel
anguish and joy shuffling hot trash mags
and a Twitter-tome about
The Body from one more academic type which gets me
scratching this into my phone—I feel like a baby crowning sliding myself
fresh through yogurt-blood though I have no child nor
will—I still sometimes half-pray to Universals

as I did when the one holy priest
spread his rheumatoid arms: "Come, eat the bread, drink the blood"
because I knew he meant the Jew Jesus, a man, a morsel
of bread, sip of wine—I taste it—way before
the Demolition of Language tried locking things down. I love

images a thousand cosmos more than *the symbol*.
Our Earth's name—"erthe," "erde," "Gaia" but
nobody yet knows the Original.
               My good doctor is entering my room
standing beside my bed "You can go home in the morning" so I know
once more it's definitely my body only mine he's talking about.

Old Red Dog

—gravel-substitute made from coal mining waste

By late July our village lost
all its money, the asphalt truck left,
and winding my way through the meadow

I'd stop for raspberries and read
inside the hawthorn, but saw something orangey-
red, our lane covered in chunks like raw meat.

Stench of rotten eggs blurred the air.
I couldn't hear a bird or see
dirt or cinder under the covering stink.

Whitman and Cather new to me
made poverty quaint-like, plentiful butter
and brown bread. Crocks of milk

thick and fresh, plank floors
gap-free, secure. I squatted beside our ditch:
bottom edges of goldenrod and blue asters

burnt and seeping acid. I felt
the mother-roots of the hawthorn
stretch down and away.

The toad holes brimmed yellow scum,
smoldering. I stepped up
onto the reddish wave, trying to cross.

Ars Poetica

Stalled and bitchy
despite this lovely loft, mine for a week;

sitting, nothing, I try
whistling: match the register

of birdcall from the high airshaft.
I scrub, sweep, releasing

the gleam of corners
when suddenly

the elevator whooshes,
a kid seven feet tall steps off

and into my space proffering a case of champagne.
Quick glance and halt: "Wrong. Sorry."

I nearly become a minor
warehouse queen,

a grace note, locket, pomegranate
intoxicating my desk

as I open the notebook
I'd given up as too nice to use.

To a New Window

Now that you're here

my eyeteeth are chewing all in sight.

Cloud cover? No problem,

I'm eating pearl and dove.

I see sand, ash, lime

you've hardened into a two-way

mirror whose cantilevers of light

pierce the base of my skull

and slide the temple door open

slipping me through time, lucky

since I wound my old watch

till it sprung, and cranked

my old window's arm till it burst.

Time-traveler, bright eye,

this morning when they set you

snug into your frame

I held my breath,

high winds were speeding

over the city's lower elevations

and kept coming closer.

You held and shine.

I can see the farthest hawthorn

on the park's upper path.

Can you take me further out?

The Ruined House

above a meadow on a high lane,
painted eggshell for years, went vacant
and grayed, most of the windows gone.

Cards and canteens, rusty cans and a camp cot
in the attic open to sky.
I counted—seven—every time I walked up there.

Three red spruce, two white pine, two hawthorn.
I knew six boys, plus my brother, who'd been
sent to Vietnam. The seven trees rimmed

the house and sang to it: wind, snowsquall,
rain and resin, thorns and pips, all their tunes
and tickings. The tarpaper roof, curled into

a funnel, made a crying sound.
The Township Draft Board protected their own.
Seven trees were singing, lifting and turning,
hiding me, going up there to scream.

An Elixir of Mica

Mother in the coal cellar

black dust and white plaster leaves sliding down.

Mother in the black and gray chiaroscuro is dying again,

calling for my brother, her first born. He

grasps her feet to steady her journey.

White plaster leaves, white breath in my cold face

in the cellar below the cellar

where I've held her a hundred times.

I lift the cold cup

I gaze down into the shimmering gray sheets of pearl

I step into the Wild Horses Mirror

where everything telescopes

and I drink.

Vernal Equinox

This night of a spring storm
I wait for the tree
to lift itself from curbside
and drift into the house.
Green perfume
sifts onto our sheets
and your sleepy head of curls.

The branches feel unlike anything
since the first time you kissed me
under the white pine
and I felt your eyelashes
on my face.

There can't ever be
our first kiss
only bare shoulders
and breathing—now
—skin and skein we stitch
   sweet resin
   sweat and teeth
   needles and fir.

Open, Grove

I have waited all summer
to come back,
cut into the woods
behind the line of sumac

thriving at the berm I walk
afternoons, unbothered.
If I've studied my girl-
hood hard, and escaped
harm (or don't remember),

if I've wept over my sister's
story and learned from it,
maybe I know either
patience or a tree's

timing. Just after first
frost, the hawthorn's
berries are ripe.
Open, grove,

holy bramble-witch
and fence, keep
small girls and boys from
falling out, keep men

from breaking in. I'll steep
the fleshy haws and brew
the tonic that fires its heart.
But no matter

how many times
I call on green, I can't
touch it.

from *The Apollonia Poems*

(2017)

Flower Meal

I slid the sliver of anchovy that holds the sea

inside the cube of robiola, and that

I slid inside the flower.

When I pinched the blossom shut

I kissed it

dipped it in egg, flour, and golden oil

then carried it on the white plate

and when you lifted it to your mouth

did you remember?

Every flower is a savant—

Only last night your mother

was waiting for you here on Via Marulena,

remember, you'd just read

the strange novel with that title

and then a word from a stranger

brought you to my table

where the jasmine loves to fall onto the dark

zucchini, so when I

with my hands   open and fill

this orange flower

have I not opened you too?

A hungry mouth,

which is voice—

and your salt-sweet restless soul?

Walking to *Miami*

—Gelateria Miami, Piazza Francesco Cucchi, 8, Rome

1.

Finish Cernuda notes   shut computer   Hydrate, grab

envelope   Ciao, Luca   avoid Louisa at curb   long stroll on twilit

Marmorata   Cross Tiber at Sublico   quick turn   drop envelope

in Eugenia's slot   Yesterday Besa told me:

    "I wanted to buy a computer? Government paperwork. Interview.

    No go." (Albanian passport and deadlined temp visa only) She's here

    ten years, brilliant student, steady at work

Graffiti tags unspool righteously against twenty-eight-percent

no/jobs/for/youth/here   like home, where our

percentages, though less, get cooked

"Distance teaches," Will Self wrote after walking to New York

from London (well, there was the plane), but he trekked the M25

Stockwell to Heathrow, flew across the pond

and walked Kennedy to Ground Zero

wedged against the guardrails

    You walked *where?*

    everyone asks my friend Patrick who walks Brooklyn

    to the Y, and Camden to Drew   "It takes time, so you have to

    map it and forget being a social sentient being."

  Turn, stop a sec, hydrate   hamstrings micro-adjust

to the seventy-four steps crenellated and complete

as if released from deep inside the Janiculum

fully formed   sudden Mobius lifting me up

into the first stirrings of night air

Men cut, carved, carried this stone

marking perfect depth of field for feet of the thirsty

climbing up to the great aqueduct   Seven sources channeled

from the countryside down and into three vast tanks

2.

From Minerva's ruined temple-marble rose Il Fontanone

    I don't "divide my time" between x and y

    Time splits me   I head up   feel the heaviness

    then I lighten, summit and stroll, and slow

    under the blueing sky before the pool

    and falls, five bays tumbling like burst spigots

    spewing escalators

    downward cooling the city

My mouth waters for the vanished

summer garden behind the iron grille,

to sit under jasmine with a silver bowl and spoon: *Cosa vorresti?*

    Some of each, my brothers would say

    all eyes on Dad opening the Sealtest

    half-gallon, pausing to display the American/

    Neapolitan block, the long knife, and the carving:

for each plate, equal slab: chocolate, vanilla,

strawberry, cross-wise   I half-circle behind the great

fountain, street still slanting upward

3.

Cross Carini—West   turn right down Francesco Daverio
He died defending the hill for the Republic

     and arrive under the pink and green neon tubes
     among starched pensioners and kids in Vans
     queuing in the doorway beneath the dayglo
         Art Deco scroll:::::*Miami*:::::

I never get why my Italian friends
fly to New York and turn left fast
for the other South
when everything here is touched by the sea

Perfume of mango   almond   tangerine   darkest chocolate *con panna*
per favore   mouth-water   Apricot because now is the season
and Italy produces the most in the EU-28

4.

Tiny port   far from Lesbos, Lampedusa, Calais, souls washing ashore
flung onto stones in hopes of safety   Our faces

reflected in the 4th World Cup 2006 posters,
faces framed and glassy, riding the surf of the hot pink wall   We inch closer

     wedges of lime   lemon wheels
     bundletts of cherries in a clay bowl beside Benedetta

who takes our orders in black stilettos and pressed black pencil skirt
immaculate lace at her clavicle framing a small silver cross

Madonna   it says, and   *Mare*

Madonna of the Sea,
    Are you lost?   Are you waiting for someone?

Benedetta rings the register
guarded by Neptune
whose marble eyes emit a bright white

Another Green

Everything got more complicated after I wrote
the four notes on scrap paper, tucked them

NorthEastSouthWest and Skip came with his pickup and icepack
of Yuenglings to help me load last things, and the sad woman pulled into the drive

would I buy a party door   a giant automated mesh garage door perfect
in summer especially like now, buggy, rain falling all this last

night   The notes I hid
hum inside the walls, I want them quiet

watching over like eyes on the street   out here where there is no street
only ex-urban speedway   once a lane of mailboxes

emptied one afternoon by a small girl   She's learning to read, opens the aluminum
doors   lowers the red flags and sorts her white dove-pets under the forsythia

reverie until mother, mailman, and neighbors arrive   She says
I'm working   but really it's a party under the wide screen

of the bush   trying to read messages of strangers without
leaving the bower's fresh green she loves more than anything.

Little Grandmother Pays an Evening Visit, Rolls Down Her Stockings and Looks Around

You want to fix something in this world? Clean your own house first.

Me? What's that bag of shoes you carry around?
If you're not wearing them, throw them out.

Can't wear shoes of the dead. You have to bury them. I want coffee.

Let me get you a shovel.

You want to make things neat in your head. Me, I read the papers.

Ha—*Jaskolka:* 1915 edition, Rzeszow's finest weekly.

Fires, money sickness, fighting there too. Here it's better. Was worst down in Shtinkin Halloh.

Sticker Hollow—named for the thorn-bushes and hawthorns along the river!
Didn't we call them jaggerbushes? Did we eat hawthorn berries?

In tea. And I found you gooseberries. I made you rose-hip for your colds.
You put honey in it. Did we eat meat-cakes?

Payday, when the bosses handed out scrip
He came all the way across the ocean
One man among many

The Poles   the Rusyns—all the Slavs the same
Who else could take 120 degrees and lift beams and crawl down holes?
Slaves—I say the word!

One among many   he ran from war   ran from the copper mines
*   so he could climb down inside Frick's shtinkin holes!*

Did you wrap his feet in newspapers in winter? Did we eat sour cream and rye bread?

Sour cream I made myself   bread I made   onions and garlic I snipped for the top
Of course I wrapped his feet

Then I went down and played with the baskets.

I let you go down to the little cellar because you were good.
This coffee is good! like mine   like tar   give me some chocolate
I let you go down to the golden onions
*   to teach you tears can be sweet*

Did we burn coal and breathe it day and night?
Did our rags turn black?

I have rags of every color—[laughs]
Ivory from bleaching   red and brown from bleedings
Green from garden   black from coughing

In the holloh house I looked down through cracks
*   in the boards and saw yellow water running from the mines*
When rains came
*   yellow water could wash us all away—*

Very Smart   Very Proud

Your mother suffered over the quickness of life
You, sad sometimes
like me,
you think you know things?

I know women will be last.
My eyes ache.

You have too many books.

I have my house, my love. Books enough for a while—

You know things?

Yeah, I know a lot of things. I know
they rape and sell girls. I know
they want to close a girls' school? Easy:
throw poison down a well.
Women, children, animals. All will be last.

Women. [Spits.]
Women cry and bleat and manipulate
I have done these things myself
    so I know!

If a woman breaks your heart, it's broken twice,
and you yourself a woman
helped it along. I've done this myself.
But

they use us. They write laws   threats   laws on our bodies   We
let them use us.
In Poland you left school before it was time, and your teacher cried.

Shut!!! I learned to read first!
Let me tell you girls and boys   old and young
All suffered
And more suffer now

Mother Comes

Was I a boy or a girl?

Both and neither. It took me a while to figure that out.

Thirty, forty years?

Long enough to know I didn't know. You burned the candle at both ends.

I've had great love affairs.

And suffered the consequences. Kto wie, daughter.

What was it with the big blue book?

Oh, everybody had that in the fifties. Your father and I got one. Even the priest knew.

Lots of pillows, positioning of the woman for the convenience of the man!

Haven't you learned anything by now?

Ha. You only taught me your idols:
Thoreau a virgin: Leopardi a virgin:
Dickinson maybe   probably not   maybe   No
wonder I was confused.

Babies are babies, the two who died I still think of.

How did you grieve?

We drove to Erie and threw our sorrows in.
We drove to Niagara and threw more in.
We drove to Chicago to the Shrine of Saint Jude. You were conceived.

Street Grate

Pocked sentry—
so many years you've looked up into the long seasons'
white-hot suns
and black-ice roofs.
Scarred bronze eye—
I wonder how many times you've seen

the fledgling screech owls'
silhouettes nightly between 10:30 and 11
on the sycamore branch above you.

8 bars across   12 down
ALLEGHENY CITY DEPARTMENT OF PUBLIC WORKS 1936
[8 pitted bronze horizontal bars/12 pitted verticals]

Smashed glass and matted rot-mouth;
rat cage-top my uncles
breathed through in the hell tunnels
they had to scrape by hand,

I hope you know the cat,
leather pads stepping
carefully   bar to bar
big fur belly hanging down
brushing you,
hole for rushing waters,
dear steel eye span.

After Reading Another Book of Dull Poetry I Go Out and Cut the Grass

Thrash blades furiously, obliterate
all, stain flagstones green

stagger to hose for cold drink, steaming,
also smeared green, eight minutes, done.
The fragrance I love? Volatiles spewing

their delicious distress call
so now I feel sad about my violence

once pouring leftover paint down the cellar
sink, burning plastic, etc. Big prize
book in today's mail so smart so icy

I ripped the cover off and tossed guts.
Usually it is very hard to write a poem

sometimes as much   sometimes far less
than Rachel Carson's labor finishing
Silent Spring, she who let her grass grow

freely up in Springdale
even when neighbors complained, she who
concurred with William Douglas
roadside flowers have inalienable rights,

who labored to simplify her book
while suffering last chemo   so the public

could read and comprehend it.
Smart poets:

Thurgood Marshall, after a hard day
on the bench loved to repair to chambers,
turn on, unwind to *The Peoples Court*.
My Subaru-sized yard is not a handkerchief of the lord

ninety percent turned over for vegetables and flowers,
but I take a sec   admire cut velvet heightening
the lilies, and the birdbath visible 360°.

Children of October

Those of us born in July, voluptuous and moody
frost the sun with our loneliness.

Under hottest skies we sing to the hidden moon.
Those born in July are children of October

carrying bushels of peaches
home, never too early to stock up, take

home wherever we go, buoyant as saltwater
showing off
our rare equilibrium
conceived in October

when two fall to the floor, laughing
in search of a lost earring.
Those of us born in July

carry our opposite season
as the willow does, she lets

long green hair down, turning flexible head
down to brush the weeds and clasp

tufts of rabbit fur into
her slender olivine leaves
dressing for the cold, always
last to drop leaves,
first to show her bittersoft mud-yellow tongues.

In an Old Hotel

In for the night I empty my pockets,
gallery stub, train card, what's left of all my 20s,
and the crushed bloom—Who placed it
in my hand, was she a new immigrant, or
a hedge-fund girl who walked into my 23rd Street
daydream and said, "Eat the body of this flower"—
What is this spiky beauty, tiny sister
to the giant pinecone pillaged for the Vatican
that Dante snarled into an enemy's prickly face?
Cone scepter in the hand of an Egyptian queen?
Maybe it's arrived
from home and the carnival of daisy-stars in our yard—
fleabane or aster or the great purplehead itself,
echinacea spinning its seed stories of the Lenape
healers who practiced its three dozen uses.
Tincture w/ goldenseal is my cold cure.
The little cone funnels me into solitude in this old hotel,
eating hours, chewing them to delicious powder,
into good work—like good hash, made by hand,
sieves, scissors. Emperor Shen Nung doled out hash
for beriberi, "female weakness," malaria, absent
mindedness in 2737 B.C. My sore eyes
and crooked Baci fingers ease while I smoke,
sweeten my enemies, myself, in my room's
unfinished wall repair, a fresco-
field I dream on while adjusting the brass
screen to my pipe, pleasure in

handling this gift of kief, carving it into dusky
blonde curls. Strike the match again and enter
another country suffused with smoky texture
of my love's kiss sending me off through the gate.

The Vowel

—Etruscan sarcophagus, Villa Giulia

I stared at her braids   afraid she was
Universal   and I was locked

   onto the earth-vowel she seemed to be mouthing
reclining at her wedding feast, hands full of grapes

   bronze bracelets aglow
    Did her mouth flute a warning

   moaning up
    through the long braids

   threading the roof of her mouth
    to the top of her head
      curving down, nape stretching into a thicket   out there—
outside the walls—?

The braids
   threaded a map   divided my head into many parts
   starched white in French braids

my mother plaited each morning
   till my eyes watered,
     I wound myself
around books

until, above half-
moon earlobes, a voice:
    You were conceived three times before you were born.

Woman on the tomb,

      Destroyer,
   to what myth
    did I first lose myself

not knowing
I was   bull-headed
and bore stone-
sounds that could
carry me anywhere?

Copper, Gold, Olives, Wine

—to Apollonia

No one way to be a woman

No one way to be a city

But I know your many cities, whether

Greek, Czech, Polish, or Slovenian,

I know your copper bracelets,

your rivers of destruction.

No way to save yourself and no one

to save you, A.D. 249 Alexandria;

Bernardino's later portrait: in your right hand

a book and colossal pincers

to vanquish torturers;

in your left, the martyr's palm frond.

Woman of no one place, Portuguese,

Brazilian, woman of Suzussa—famous

crayfish and wine! Of Sozopol,

Pontica, and Pollina Sicilia,

so many places bear your name;

you are honored here too:

bowl of olives and oil, glass with a worn

gold rim, in this house built on Pennsylvania

soil, old earth, many times over

burred and extracted.

Apollonia Is Restored to the Book

We already know
why Anonymous did not step forward
to speak
to sign her canvas:

(adultery   rape and shame   abortion
burials   slanders of forgery, parody, plagiarism;
worst: shyness of her own genius)

but my Apollonia
was bound to a young Polish soldier
from the Vistula, sent to Italy, War of 1866.

Her birth name carried from Pollina,
north, east via Bari, and Turkey, east
to the green-cold Carpathians.

Who removed her name
from the ledger of the old church?
Who penciled it back in?

from *The Water Books*

(2012)

New Black Dress

I slip it over my head and step out into dusk

softest time on the planet, feel its weight and folds

Streetlamps are turning themselves on

like relaxed insomniacs,

evening releases its green sugar and white oils

Glide the car onto the Boulevard of the Allies and admire

the windows silver-foiling their reflections of the Hot Metal Bridge

Would it be nice   to go from youth straight to death

no thin hair   loose teeth   no mind-slipping   just the rag bin

What's possible   pleasure of a simple dress

neckline to hem

the body of the shift

floating above the shift-gears of the night rivers

where otters slide onto their backs

in the deep Monongahela again

their eyelashes filtering silt from liquid   near from far

maybe a keyhole view of a deep black dress

holding another creature also

silk   fur   bone

Could I wear this dress till its cottonsilk

grows into my skin   corpse dress

its fine cinder-black ground to ash

Pack light   move on

with all who travel by river or sea

What's possible   latitudes—Pittsburgh:

40 degrees, Rome: 41—not so far-off

if parallel lines meet in space   but I miss my new friends,

won't see them for two years

Their gift of a dress

folded into a paper sleeve and mailed

from Monteverde in time for

now　Tonight belongs to her new moon body

with its translucent hem running

the circumference of its black rhinestone tail

Field Near Rzeszow

—family field in the Carpathians originally passed down through the line of women

> *How I had thought*
> *this field, that meadow*
> *is branded for eternity—*
> —H.D., "R.A.F.," 1941

If these young rye flowers
stand up every summer
then fall under grindstones
and fists of bakers,

if the stalks return to earth, rough,
return green every Spring,
    and if the ditches the aircraft wheels made

exist only in a censored photograph
    and in grass-tracings above tiny black *allées*
        down where worms make their tracks

why am I standing on an open balcony
dreaming for my own land,
    and hers before me?

        Two men play guitars
down in the street on the edge of town
    and sing about the sky—
        say, then shout, *niebo*
in a high laughing song, then
a woman's voice interrupts, in English,
    I see the back of her head

which looks tired, but she sounds intent,
we are all shouting.

I wish I knew Polish well enough
to hear the song again,

backstitch whose sky
whose field, and who owns
the fern banks across the field.

If I really owned this land
I would like to lie down on it through thirty seasons.

Go into the woods
get the black dirt
for the flowerpots.

Save the brown water
from the sinks and tubs,
save the dregs of the soup pot
for the geraniums,
save the coffee grounds for the roses.

Dig for the best nightcrawlers
under the shadows of boulders
at the edge of the meadow where the table-
rock piled with the big rocks
writes its story in long lines—

I would do these things.
I would study the scars
and glyphs the moraines clawed
in granite and limestone when the mammoth
plates scraped the land. When they stopped
moving they left overhangs and ledges,

rock-niches for rock-rose.
        I get the hair-on-the-back-of-the-neck sensation
    at the edge of a field
            and like to read
    in the grass of a ditch
where weeds show
        spit-pockets inside their blades,
    and the thatchings give groundcover
        to pebbles usually brown and black and sometimes a white
quartz fragment sits there reflecting
        light up into the bird and butterfly paths.

Snakes, insect clouds, rabbits
    must like the heat of earth at that
            close range. And the tall blue

flowers rimming the deer beds—
            like hairlines.
Don't
    work late,
        the field spirits come out at dusk—
            Night lasts all night.

Not much to go on, my field's war-time biography—
the photo:
a simple field stolen *x* times over.
Unseal it and see:

the original wedding gift,
the furrows turned,
moist, open.

One word, *niebo*,
translates part of the song:

If I say I like your *niebieska* blouse
I mean *blue*.
    When I say
the only *niebo* for me
is the one above my family field
I am calling it heaven.

On the Tarmac at Dover Air Force Base

—April 2006. The eighteen-year ban on media coverage of returning
American war dead was lifted by Obama in 2009.

The sodium vapor lights look down
inside their columns of rain
and light the hot pavement sending its
steam back up. Drops of oil and rain
    smeared by a truck, drops the size of dimes,
me looking for something
to focus on: a feather, a shoelace tip,
a comb, a rusting
    stencil I find in a storm ditch:
        1   2   3   ZERO—
an honor guard—
    Rain eyes—
    cameras.

Under the scrims of grease, in rainwater
    you might catch a glimpse of something
    human, or mechanical,
simple acts of love and
friendship seeing the dead
on a daily basis
in their transport.

Our tongue
and soil
twist themselves in a lost key,
    the dark and the quiet are going to have to be enough
    space for thinking.

I had to sit
out under the stars last night: accidental lockout
on my porch looking in, and I prepared
to come here, see the runway, the hangar,
all the empty parking spaces where TV trucks
should be. I lost
my key, I'd left the news on,
the windows were sealed,
the evening star was blinking,
the dead show up no matter what; in the cemetery
at Frick Park you can look inside the little
houses even the rich don't visit, leaves and webs
unswept, the Tiffany glass unpolished; down the hill
endless rows of stones
     another on another in a crooked wedding
     cake of white stones high as rowhouses,
gray stones patinaed with soot, photos
of the dead under glass.

Milosz said we can't have Earth, can't
even attain it in our dreams;
what harm in coming here
seeing how and who we kill? I can't
give anything but memory,

only the eyes
might see through
the cinder layer
     the clay level—
     the mineral kingdom
     upside down.
Only the living
come to pick up their young
coffins.
     Here's a leaf: almond shaped

with water droplets, rinsed, leathery.
Stomping in creeks—
    some of the boys did that—
and the girls, some made dishes from catalpa leaves
    and served flower meals on them, washed their hands
with leaves after feeding their doll families.
The thought of boots in creek beds,
leaf-picnics and water
      taking the crisp top layer of the leaf,
softening it,

the thought of boot leather softened by rain, scratched by mud.

Here on asphalt having no one to greet,
having no one to bury, bless my luck in this hour.
The dead soften inside the coffins
under the medals and the censored grief.

To a Lamp

Little moon on a silver pole
no rock will smash you on my watch

no ghost-whistle from the sad streets
of Trafford Westinghouse will scold *Go home*

no profit-siren yowl *Hurry, before you lose*
all the hours you owe us

I love your single eye-
globe of filaments

lighting the cross-hatched shrubs,
gate-posts welded at their notches

Only you, satin crookneck
brighten the ochre bricks made of clay

dug from the riverbanks
When the ambulance comes to take him

I'll have to turn back
and find my way past windows

splintering light into rings and chains
along the sidewalk between night's

floor and ceiling where this new
grieving absorbs and stores me

under the gentle attendance
of your illumination

Sticks Found in a Ravine

Kindling, a bonfire in honor of Pasolini

who prayed to his own mother, cursing and thanking her for too much love.

His film critiques gave me a headache but his

Decamerone changed my girl-life, seeing the lover cup her hand on her man's

cock, both sleeping on an open porch.

Up here in the Pamphilii woods I'm leaving a hobo prayer stick for Pasolini, and

one for Jimmö, destroyed in the first wave of AIDS. I can never find Pasolini,

but the *Roman Poems* helped my first efforts. They do now.

It was my mother's love

let me slide my tongue inside the slit of a woman. Suck a man clean.

I can't find you in Via Carini's sweet queer *passiagata*.

Didn't find you among Testaccio's crushed lamps and bones.

In your time

boys run to you for bags of oranges and bread.

Boys you run to for love, and vanish in smoke and hunger.

A few of these words sting with sweet salt

from this gay life neither you nor I

fully embrace.

Say the body beautiful *wherever it falls on the slippery continuum,*

you wrote. Your Friulian, your local-rough dialect

busted the Italian canon wide open.

Dear famous lovechild.

My Orange

Take one
from the basket
with the cup of bittersweet coffee, this is all
I'm going to get this morning because
Vittorini is teaching me again another membrane

of truth so do not repeat
my spendthrift days, the ones that went
uneaten, little suns on my bookshelf
dried up pulp and laces.
Now when I try for greater focus
every plate means something and yes there's no
food in *The Charterhouse of Parma* because Stendhal was obese,
maybe punishing himself, now there's another new war
and time is so tight. Now bend my thumb

angle it down through the oily skin
of the globe, thank
the old cast-offs
tucked into the toes of the Christmas stockings
(I was digging for Kennedy halves
and the walnuts and chocolates). In the lunch box
I wanted concentrate
or the horrible Tang
the astronauts packed into space—Though we're known

throughout the world
for our bombs,
our baskets glow with the light
of a thousand miles of trees
and the human
fingers of the pickers
burnt with the sweet acid.

Hole in the Sky

The dead ascend to heaven through white holes
into blue and that is why The Virgin's robe
was blue, the priestdrone easy to believe until
she died
who fed and combed me
with the callused palm of her hand. When she died
I hid under the cellar steps
shredding the hem of my skirt,
it calmed me to see colors in the weave.
The sky sucked her up, Reverse Hell, it was icy
and lonely, the sucking tornado hole of it
took her from the other hole
no one stayed to see the dirt packed onto.
I was going up through the hole
I thought, sitting under the steps
and ceiling vents with all the other
houses along the old boulevards and alleybacks
facing the yellow rivers
and the huge rushes and mists furled
upward, escapes always up into the sky. I look
up and she's still alive to me
but not her
human world of steel buckets   sour boots and septic
fractures in the foundations and men
blowing their noses into their fingers.

Kinzua

*—northwestern Pennsylvania, on the eve of construction
of Seneca Allegany Casino*

The ground is wet and cold
where we abandon ourselves
to Alice Cooper and the Scorpions and set the tents
and central firepit circled by stones; we bring
the good knife from the Subaru's side-door compartment
and two days food, tarps, wine;
        breeze sifts through spruce,
  I adjust the screen over the fire, brew the Yukon
    fine-grind, and roll a celebratory and elegiac
       joint while late frost

begins its sweat-melt under the Aries sun
    and something gray and unlabeled by clouds: sky
opens at the edge of the water;
    skunk cabbage switchblades
    release their stench.

       Sharp smoke
draws wavy lines around our space so we don't
    see the bobcat slip over the berm and climb the ridge

    accompanied by ghosts tamping messages
        deeper into the bulldozed trails;
we're fireside, early,
      exhilarated and solemn
        up here in the last of it.

The Bowl

I saw under water between two rocks a small round bowl made of clear ice, interior concave smoothed, reflecting morning.   Where the bowl came from, how it wedged itself here, who could feed from it, perfect for chilling fruit in July, for icing coffee with a dollop of sugared snow, I don't know. But the someone that might pluck it out of the water and set it over there on the flat rock, or carve it into spoons for a meal on that table, has left it here, under a thin membrane of water,   preserving its fine shape and crystals. Rather not ask or disturb this instrument, place-mark, or lens I might lift to read the water books.

For Aaron Sheon

"Tiny hatches, if you make enough of them, make

an entire etching move," you told us while we smoked

in the lit cave of your Tuesday 1–2:15. We scratched

our pens: dance and film posters, flyers to end the war.

In our famous jeans we slouched before your podium and slides weaving

the movements, the solo trips.

"He was lonely." "She had no patron."

"Scale extends us and reins us in," you said of the strange Piranesis.

"Find the heart of a city by stepping in."

My alleys and arcades pressed onto the copperplate of my twenty-year-old brain

fusing its hemispheres.   I hitched to Colmar and found

the Isenheim Altarpiece, figures on the old panels aflame, then turned

my back on all religions because you'd shown us Goya's firing squad and Daumier's gutters where people looked for water.

"Movement in a painting is important as Dante."

I've looked for Dante's houses, cafés, notebooks, and horse-stalls, and someone

always says   *Oh, you mean The Poet.*

"The body doesn't make sense by itself," you said, pointing the red-tip

wand at the chalky nudes of Ingres. If I am lonely

in any town whose museum

treasures its one Whistler or Bonnard, I stand before the image

and hear your voice; my eyes

unscroll, I lift

again like a hinge.

I Take My Mother to See the Rothko Panels, 2007

—and she recites from Polish folklore

Her eyes are adjusting
like heat-sensors on low
in the dim gallery.

It's all touch; she leads,
her thin arm steers down, four steps,

another ten to the soft banquette, but we say bench,
    and laugh at the old joke: her mother after a social call:
    "And what did she give you?" (it was the Depression:
    coffee, a roll?) "A bench to put my ass on."

We find ourselves
    in a dark room warm with paint, cool with stone.

That house was so reliable—Oh
he must have painted these at night.

In that house when you said goodnight you said
"Sleep red, sleep white," depending
on where you slept: the fire room, the white room.

These look more like stains than paint.
We had soot for conservation,
soon as the roof tiles
wore out on one side
we turned them over and nailed them back down.

Her mother's house on the banks of the Vistula
was bordered with willows and firs,
their greens brushed by weather.

She pulls us to breath-distance of the canvas
    so close we wash ourselves down
    in crimson and sienna, Rothko's Pompeii.
    He spiked his commission for the grand restaurant
    with "something that will ruin the appetite
            of every son-of-a-bitch who ever eats in that room."

We find ourselves in a room beamed by fire and stars.
    He must have painted these at night
        to get the maroons and oranges this warm.

During windstorms we thought the house walked,
it swayed like it was on springs,
bending in the winds and then
it came back to its original position.

    In a dark room beamed by fire and stars
    My grandfather stepped up onto the ladder—

he used cross-bars and sealed the beams
with forest moss, and later, wool.
Even the attic slats were shaped like sunbeams.

In the white room they had religious
pictures painted on glass.
He carved the sun
and the rosette, a star, up near the roof.

Entering

—for Vera, in search of the sheela na gig
(ancient Irish vulva) in Rome

I feel the curvature, but barely;
entering the city on stone cold radials
    that stretch and extend themselves
   out from the cervix of the center
   among thousands of centers, I look up

high along a balustrade the ancient carved almond, *mandorla*,
the almond-slit, *vesica piscis*,
   the death-woman opens her legs and holds,

so all see while they're walking and looking up
the open muscles and lips
casting (what?)

down on smartcars, buses, bikes, carts, wheelbarrows
the swollen massive rosettes of the birther-to-all-men
life-cunt dripping onto
streetcars' silver-hot tracks—

Once young women squatted over the open furrows:
   bountiful harvest

My own yoni heart
   sheening itself with so much touching:
   moist tentacles of the vicoli I twist inside of

I nod to the old woman almond
    crumbling;
      above, a fresh tag:
        Stop beating women

This walk my feet were made for:
    the flight, bag, coat I dropped
        coming back to the Via Giulia

on a Monday morning in May
        moving past the excavations and
displays of the dead

After Pavese's "Grappa in September"

No laziness like mine, little crystal cup,
tomatoes canned, late basil crushed to pesto.
Nothing better than 95 degrees in the shade.
People like us don't sweat in the heat because we work.
The sun finds a place on our skin and has no need to make it shine.

from *Reactor*

(2004)

The Coffee Line

—after the painting by John Sloan, 1905

The cart was a house we approached at dawn,
the man tended the chrome pots bent over
in his canvas apron, the steam a circuit above the boiling
water and the smell could knock you out at 6 in the morning;
our paper bags softened in the mist, and our lunches sealed
in waxed paper held meats and fruit—
second sweetness of the day—but this would be the first, the dark
poured into our thermoses, the dark warmed our faces
in the first-light, the smell, holy
smell of the whole oiled and turning world
smoked into our nostrils down onto our tongues,
eyes in our heads watered, ears opened
to the sound of pouring from the chrome spout,
the falling dark waterfall into the cup, 1 cup
now before work, sipping the dark, 2 sugars, 3,
help yourself to a 4th, it's payday,
the milk warmed if possible   is that possible, the man
bends toward us, hands up the cup and keeps pouring
elixir and frugality, cost and profit. Every morning
the red ring of the single burner on the white
stove in the cart can be seen from far away in the black
wet streets we walk, minds dipped in sky-tar
buffed to something ebony and bony and vase-like;
we walk toward the wedding ring of night and morning fused,
Saturn, ring of the brain's tiny volcanoes awakening.

from Yucca Mountain Sequence

i. The Reactor

The dome of heaven was built in a single frame.
—MARINA TSVETAYEVA

I didn't care for my brothers' toys,
even the silver cities that rose under the piano
were part of another stage. I wanted the gray tower
fitted from 500 pieces, the model someone
designed for whom, unclear; my brothers
placed it, finished, on the gameroom table,
and rejoined their camp in the woods. Someone must
know the code to its tiny red door; someone walked
its halls and polished the white floors,
the Deerfield River ran beside it,
we saw a movie on summer vacation.
Pipes big as tunnels shined plain steel. Something flowed
out of the tower and into the cold river
and over the bright scales of fish.
Tower with slipper sides,
dome without windows,

I studied your gray skin
then one day made myself small enough
to climb the curved ladder over the skull and down
the other side, I could see the door, the halls,
and the men in white paper suits. I took it
to school, it would be my own Taj Mahal,
palace for a princess, men in paper-white suits

would make light and heat for all the nations. My prince built the creamy white
halls for love and laid blue tiles for the pool
of golden carp. The people would walk the graveled paths a thousand years.
every walk a walk of sadness, yes, their princess was dead, but also
a walk of awe every day in her presence. See the swans and peach trees along
the river that flows beside it. See the terrible silver rods
and pipes filled with poison through the glass
but you never have to touch them,
the plutonium is slippery and will burn
the flesh off your hands. This is the way
we open the tiny red door and walk inside but

it was only a model after all and not the real
palace where the men stood over the silver-black pool balancing pipes the size
of tunnels, and rods delicate as the bones of deer.
The princess was wrapped in her ivory skin
and black black hair braided with pearls and ribbons.
The people went to gaze into the blue water
and to imagine touching the cool fins of the golden fish.
They gathered rose petals and feathers of red and yellow birds. Dome,

slick shell, labor of love, architect's untouchable
model, my schoolmates looked politely and couldn't see

I would have peeled you open just to see your fire.

ii. Sedan Crater, 1962–

I love this place, it is restful.
  —DEREK S. SCAMMELL, ex-limo driver to The Beatles, triple-tour Vietnam veteran,
  and National Nuclear Security Administration guide to the then-proposed U.S. nuclear
  waste repository at Yucca Mountain; in the outback of the Nevada Test Site, October 2001

What are you breathing: pine:
Eastern white? Sugar of the Sierra
Nevada? Important to know the difference.

I have a mocha eye

There are buses at the gate, catch the diesel on the wind.
A young man is fixing his badge and the sinking feeling after donuts and coffee.

Are you breathing eye talc,
taupe silk brushed across the lid—
briefcase packed for your daily test?

A scratch of mesquite arrives in my ragged wind
Are you far

from 32 men per bus, 11 buses on their way to an elevator
deep as the Empire State Building?
Up from Vegas and Henderson the miners ride,
men of the Sheep Range and nightless casinos;
one is looking out the tinted window at beige
on a 2-hour ride. Before gunpoint-check and piss test
he's gazing at the curved places in the caliche:
he could crawl in
while the sun's still mild, the Sheep glint
by 8:42 sharp. He has another hour's
ride, the 15 minutes down.
Boney piles of the East, he wouldn't know you. He's carving
a new room for the silver coin of plutonium

arriving tonight in a classified white-on-white truck.

Vats of the thing that never dies,
are you far?
    Old bomb clouds
    Plumb-bob and Charlie, Buster-Jangle and Plowshare—

—ghosts that travel the wind
I'm four football fields wide and twice that underground

A blue sky
then voices come over me

Very wide, very light here

    What are you breathing: lilac
or syringa?   Random sagebrush perforate my photographed circumference

Everything you couldn't see
blasted by the switch
got sucked down

Millions
of flutes—bones, feather-stems
claws, and lungs   Every creature in my range

    The lizard in Mr. Stafford's poem
    had to wait at the edge of the desert
    trembled there

A miner can't look out a window for long,
he has to go down

Here comes the dusty start of a rain
Make a mocha cake
Make a pool

down inside the thing that doesn't die,
the dull sand-metal. Even simple coins of mica,
by comparison, glint
like cat's-eyes

And what pitch does the wind
make over me so softly?
Mojave, important
above my mocha eye

iii. U1A Tunnel: Persephone's Story

I have to keep the walls dry,
generators smooth, their nerves
are real porcupines! Keep the streets
from cracking, the sand
blows heavy above. Once I was
a woman, actually 2, in white dresses,
I lay dead, my mother wailed
over my body, then I was alive,
singing, there were gems, also
white: calcite, pearl, opal, druzy.
Now I am another.
Pipes and wire form the grid;
cable shapes the dome. Crust
protects our fortune, which is
slippery. See,
this new room painted cottage red
isn't a landfill or tomb—it's
a lab, future for the nation,
which turned, momentarily, to
Poetry, the Pope, Bono, etc.
after the last rupture. Now it's
another, too. Here's the pyro-
chiller, the diagnostic alcove.
I don't miss myself—this is home now—

Here is kismet—
lovely marine blue. Climb
the red ladder of light,
see the water for yourself. This
is the fortune.

vi. Abandoned Camp Near Paiute Mesa

Out in the fallen corral

among stones a pocketful of stones

clustered in the sand:

blue-gauze water of bright turquoise.

Coffee with Narrative

Voltaire's 70 cups to my 2,
what does that make me, though
his we think were demitasse and mine
are big as small dogs. How no one
smokes anymore, sad, I open my pack
here in the night kitchen and out comes
exotic Mlle. Teuer, laughing, black cat
on her shoulder, and I rivet on her cup
of sugar-tar while she smokes into the night
and regales me with her vanished minor opera-
star years, drops of holiness wetting her smock.
If I run my hand along this shelf I slide into a farmstead
where I drank the green, the black teas,
organic leaves picked from bushes in far places
no longer far. But the beloved sister
to cabernet and cognac, to mountain water over matching
ice cubes would be the gift of Ethiopia
that would transmogrify Earth.
Dear red berries who made goats dance about,
dear leaf veins turgid and erect, how
the little goats peed on those bushes, thus
deepening the primal blend
Dante to Beauvoir:

Books are wires and nerves lined up and tangled
in the starry intelligence of our evolution:
Achievement in American Poetry/Miss Bogan
praised our young literature grand as Interstate 80

running East/West through the basins and ranges
woolly mammoths ran. This road trip
packs square cheeses, paints, sheets, towels,
and celebrates friends, not tidy aesthetes:
"The personal voice is dead."
"Accessibility is dead."
Birds zoom down to the Bluegrass following paths,
might reincarnate, might not, humans will
eradicate them, might not.
The experiment occurs
and I am the experiment.
Dickens got meta-psyche 100 years before Barthes:
"*I* know your tricks and your manners," said Jenny Wren.
    "*I* know where you've been to." I got Marx
on uneven development
because a nun who was mean hungover
spelled it out in plain English.
    The summer I made
a strange series of exits, everyone thought
I was bereft, without love; I was, I couldn't
hear The Sirens, those eyelined
intellectuals chatting at sidewalk tables
so in-the-moment. I was the silver locket
at that one's throat, I was the brown disc inside
that one's cup. I couldn't stop slipping
into a new skin. How would I recognize myself?
I am the experiment.   When I woke up in Pennsylvania

Mała Babka poured me a cup of hot milk and then
into it poured a cup of hot coffee.
Every summer evening she scattered the day's grounds
under the geraniums and roses that bloomed 50 years.
I bled a bloody heart of Jesus for love, an old story,
but it was new to me. The story we must tell
we tell. I like pre-writing, housework in general,

as now I'm digging dirt from the kitchen tiles
with my fingernail. This morning,
on the other hand, I'm traveling
light or, you could say, free.

In Praise of Camus at the End of His Century

Paper comes from trees, wine comes from the grape,
I love my country. Today came in two distinct parts

instead of one vat of moments. In the first part
I read without interruption, and in the second

I had time to think through some things. Like you,
all the writers in America have been looking for their fathers.

You'd like this view: white mist over the Adirondacks.
Fly-fishermen wade the dark blue Ausable,

first day of season. Beginnings: the idea we stay in love with.
I looked at the "new urbanism" photos down in the city; impossible

to know if the streets are dead or living; Teenie Harris is better, so
is Stieglitz, *a kind of old American Socrates.* And the small retrospective

of Souso-Cordoso, exiled in '44, whose masked fantasy-rabbit leaps
through sci-fi foliage and monstrous pools: nature weds tech

and survives, camouflaged. *Now there are a lot of things
that artistically speaking I know I could* make work. *But this no longer*

means anything to me. There's war in Algiers again,
kids and their mothers are pulled through doors and slaughtered.

I wish I knew the small inn you visited up here in the North Country
in 1946, I would take flowers . . . *the simplicity of the room, the remoteness*

of everything, make him decide to stay there permanently, to cut all ties with
what had been his life and to send no news of himself to anyone. I like working

in this cabin along the river, writing near water: plenty
and lack, Earth's greatest mystery. Hiking this morning I wanted to

lie down in the Ausable and turn into a blue-green plant,
tuning out the *ME*s. I brought your journals—one new; and my old

grad school copy, scratched with my embarrassing
margin notes: "the advance of art and empowerment of women

would end all war." My brutal country grows more isolate and frenzied,
we have all these demons: 1) cannot connect to social transformation

because money is oxygen; 2) oxygen supply visibly controlled by 3%.
In '46 you were little more than half my age now,

though you've always seemed—forgive me—
like my slightly older brother: moody like me, in love with the sea,

wandering in a mildly delirious loneliness. As you've noted,
in America we tend to wear anticipated tragedy like a badge.

Some are drowning some are sleeping. Enraged mirror-portraits
of our kids keep showing up in faces of the young

all over Earth. *This big country, calm and slow. One feels it has been*
completely unaware of the war. You were exhausted, touring,

happiest shipboard, serene staring out over the water.
I've mastered two or three things in myself. The rock shapes out my window

make good company, the spruce winds are astringent.
I'm sitting by a fire and finally, who I am, another question not worth

answering. It has rained all evening. My cabin smells of balsam.
The wine carries a deep ruby color and is delicious.

Port of Entry

The world breathes
its generous display: You can have this! And this!
Look mama, a fish tail a child cries at the icy
seafood window, and in the blip before hearing
her mother's *Yes!* she's gone, time
is silk, burning, eyes out of nowhere open petals, pages
—she's through, she's peeking
onto the tip of the flat-wavy cosmos,
a world rushes forward and up through
her feet, palms and fingertips.
Ecstasy,
move us, each first time.

Installation

The men on the bridge might not be men,
they might be boys glazed hard, bleached out.
They slouch like wiry rock techies. This is all a show
This is no show   They might not stand up to time, to work
the way some paintings can. They're too easy. Who are they.

        Some drop
coins into the cup of the one I'll call the lead.
He cursed me last week as I passed, blank. Then I saw the dogs.
They lie in dead sleep while the lead and his men hold the bridge.
He's working, asking each person he can for money.
Today I stopped. There was only one small dog,
there had been four. Where are your dogs, I said.
This is the only one we have now, he said.
Did the others run off? Yes, that's what happened.
His eyes were wet blue. He smiled a vacation breeze.
I felt a hole in him ten feet deep.

        The dogs sleep
like the dead, heads down, paws and tails out
slack exactly because they are up all night
keeping guard over these boys who feed them
run them ragged.

She Kept Me

wrapped and close and fragrant
in her incense of strange lemon soap.
She carried me down, all the way down
into her solitude, lace and bones was all
she was under the t-shirt
faded to watered black silk, thin
as her night veils, dreams

of wet earth, spring, Amsterdam
where she hung with the houseboat boys,
loading bricks of blond hash safely on;
she nursed their sore throats with concentrations
of aspirin and oranges. Spent her money on
art cards and books with blue wrappers.
Whores in windows moved
their lips like bright candies
and petals drifted down

onto my woven shoulders
and the three weeks we had,
hotels, of course, also her parents'
canal-side perch where I held her
while she read her Stendhal, her Colette,
the stitches of my devotion
weight she counted on
for *quiet, let's find the exact point of focus, now that's desire,*
isn't it? O it is sex, mother
of all creative energies, books, and companion views.

I liked her
in the cool air of her balcony nights.
I was left on a train and once in a musty café.
I was handed down, yes, but never
taken up so fondly.

Spill

Before, I spoke of clear things,
shadows on white tile, men in paper suits
mopping the radiated water with Kotex pads
trucked in through the security dock, 1960. Now
I see blurry grasses swaying in dusk, the starless
sky and vaporous shapes of a Pennsylvania
town behind wire fences, there in the misty
place beyond the woods. I hear a truck
sputtering with cheap gas, and boot soles
slapping cement. *Is that my Uncle Ray*
running toward the truck, away? No, he's inside
with his men cleaning the burning place
protecting the core. Dawn is a swollen eye
they work toward. Those must be cattails
waving over the marshland, those must be geese
making that slapping leather sound of flight.

Note to the Mist

—at H.D.'s grave

I belong to you,
    O nonhuman mind, scarf knotted at the throat,
     my mind's a sax, brass gone smoky.
          I could call you
spider web blown in from Palermo,
    but we're in a different town. Good to lunch
    on bread and sharp yellow cheese a few blocks from Bethlehem
    Steel, very good to read
    one more page of Baudelaire
            to her,
Greek flower

    All flowers are roses,
      even you, mist,
unfold your pearlescent lips from the black trees.
    Your shreds and veils are blocking my peripheral vision
      but I see through you, I'm writing on you,
my blue ink's running blue.
    The December pines are still waiting for snow
    or bending for something fluctuating
    and changing colors.
    I brought thick paper for a grave rubbing, but
    your wet kiss floats me up a hillside,
    you're making the mountains bigger, closer. Which jade cloud
opened up a thousand miles north?
           Which far waterfall
sent your organza veils?

When London fell around her,
when the rails were ripped out of their tracks
and melted for guns
she thought about running away,
         on wealth, and love's vapor.

Astronomer's daughter, single mother, untranslatable
    seer, senser of vibrations on the windscreens
    that move our lives,
    behind a slightly open door

she is sitting and practicing the hard
facts of her vocation.
         Good when the gatekeeper
waved me in to the serpentine
    and casually pointed
    the exact pathway to her.
    Some of the men (and later, women too)
hated "the American Virginia Woolf"
    for the hush of servants, the child
    ushered away from mother's study. *We all could get our work done*
    if we had that kind of money. Enough.

I belong to you,
O nonhuman mind,
I'm dissolving and oxidizing
    in the brain of your strange movements
that come and go in this mild air.
    When I got out of the car I was walking around in a daze
    through the chalk-white paths and matte greenways toward

this white stone   her words on it
and blood dampening my jeans, no kidding, my assumed
    last and final menses
    replicated. This morning I dreamed I was walking
along a balustrade, Pittsburgh falling all around me

no place to go
so I sat down at my desk and worked.
Who can hold onto the safehouse of quiet work?
Where is she gone to,
mist, little house of silver pencils, little grappa bench I sit on,
gray day like a porch
sandpapered down to wood grain,
to skin, to the fire inside me?

from *The Door Open to the Fire*

(1997)

My Sublimation

I wasn't talking about the trees,
I was talking about the drive through the Corliss Tunnels
and the cinder trail leading into Fairywood
in the West End where under fog that falls
like spoonfuls of gray sorbet
Pittsburgh stands in for Paris, San Francisco,
a minor, gritty Rome—look at the seven hills,
the parapets and mushroom towers,
the rivers' pewter blades chopping the wharves.
Freud was more than
a little off, none of this is larger than life.
Bridges drip benzene and Neville Island is something you don't
want to look at, well, maybe from the air.

Take the art away from the artist
and we have a crazy person, the great man said.
Take away the gothic Union Trust masterpiece
and you have the Alcoa Building and its crenelated aluminum
of the fifties. The mild narcosis
of the Golden Triangle seen from the air
is our vulva, our hieroglyphic opening
to the nine-mile stream winding its oiled black veins
under our streets.

Do statues really move at night?
Have those who point down at us
from the Carnegie and who lounge on their forearms
along the rivers merely been visiting all these years?
Whatever's fragrant this evening when we walk back

to our cars and houses is carried on the wind
from the Laurel Mountains.
There's one stand of goldenrod along the fence
at Neville Island. I forgot
the stifling breath goldenrod can fill a room with.

After 235 years you can get a decent cappuccino in Pittsburgh.
We don't know yet what this means but we know it's a lie
to say art has replaced steel
or that many writers have work. We do know
the categorization of everything has arrived here too.
Your friend shows up at a party wearing a cocktail dress with a leather jacket
somebody's bound to say, *Where'd she come from?*

It would be cheaper to abandon Pittsburgh than rebuild it,
Frank Lloyd Wright said. Then again
he designed Fallingwater without a decent chair
to sit in. I live inside this town
so this is how I talk.
You can write about rivers all you want
but the truth is
most people here
have never touched the water.

Asleep at the 2001 Club, Early Seventies

The dead hunting
and the alive, ahunted.
—FRANK O'HARA

The boys were in the bathroom doing poppers
and tabbing their scores: six, eight, ten fucks that night
in a modest city far from the Castro or Key West.
Hating disco
I sat out another dance
while everybody else got it on, all body no mind
(my problem, no one else's).
The drag queens were lovely in their dark gloves
and strapless gowns, but I was drowsy
meaning high so I lay down under a long
corner table, first to watch two beautiful kids grind—
but lightly, lightly into each other's crotches
and what joined them till their
cocks strained, sculpted—I fell into

my persistent dream
of the bacchantes
who in their equal passions for wine and dance
snaked and leapt inside their circle till they lost
consciousness one night in the town square
of Amphissa, city at war with their home
district, Phocis. The old women of Amphissa
stood guard over their dance and their collapse
till dawn, then offered them food and wine
before escorting them out of town.

123

When I woke up I didn't know
what to do but I tried
to make a painting, a fresco
out back on my garage wall
where the molds are ripe and thick.
I designed it at the last minute after hours
of lying on my couch doing nothing
then executed it quickly, at the last minute,
then finished it with fish and shells,
platters of fruit, bread and cheese
and strong coffee because morning
carries the darkness and bittersweet
resins of the night before.

The bacchantes were neither goddesses nor special,
they were who they were, revelers, 500 B.C.
who wore the skins of leopards to celebrate
their speed and grace. Who loved breaking
the skin of the grape, and dancing and the heavy sleep
that came after. I love them
for their open beauty
and transparent pleasures,
the human being alert to its physical character
without interference.
   Where is the red-haired boy?
Gone to Cleveland and the string of fifty lousy jobs.
Now he's buried, ashes flung into the sea.
Where's the black-haired guy who played Strider,
the secret protector of Middle Earth,
who'd straddle a barstool
then whirl off
like a magnificent feline prince?
Now he's buried, bones quilted to roots and stones.

I didn't see them when they went down. For years
they favored my breakfast table or rode the passenger
seat to the liquor store. For years they talked
while I was talking, or their faces stared
at mine, insomniac. Which is what the dead do.
Do you believe that? I drew on that, I'm sucking
on it now. I could no more
escort them to a safe place
than I can read a topographical map
or cry without making sounds.
We were friends
and held the door open to the fire.

Poem at an Unmarked Grave

Your grave is untouched by flowers
I might have brought.
You left me this fierce love of spaces.
My newest memorial to you
is a meadow garden holding stones
of many shapes: mushroom, serpent,
loaf of bread. You enter through the East
and spiral through it
till you come to two log chairs.
It's stunning
the way wind through the pines
still can't make the sound of your voice.

"Everyplace is like everyplace," you'd laugh
those nights we stayed enchanted
till dawn at your drafting table smoking
and drawing boulevards and libraries.
Your front windows above the glinting intersections
were the eyes I used: the body
of Pittsburgh curved under snow,
sculpted finally into our dreams of it, whole,
the public domain of the universities and factories
met the sturdy chimneys and streets of our privacy.
We were twenty and lived inside Emerson's miracle:
a college education is a room with a fire
inside a strange city.

The Sound of the Slap

I've carried the scream
all afternoon in O'Hare.
Maybe I'm the only person
carrying the sound

from the ladies room where I found her
bracing herself against the cold tile wall
hiding from her mother

her mother's voice insistent
calling her for medicine and cleaning
calling her to the sink.

I walked in as the woman with well-dressed hair
and well-fed body pulled her child by the hair
slapped her full across the face then shoved

the medicine stopper into the twisted mouth
while the child screamed and tried to move.
Inside my stall I could hear other women

running water and tearing paper, then clicking out
avoiding the mirrors
where the woman held on to her child,

now cleaning, now stopping to slap
the red nutmeat of her face.
The skin of my cheeks stings.

I'm just one person
but I have a mouth
but I said nothing.

Passing the Clinic in a Small Town

marigold, flower of worry
—ROBERT DESNOS

I don't have to climb those steps
between fists of graffiti
and I don't have to walk through the door
and sit and be interviewed by a fearful woman
who will ask me when
and how did I fail.
The woman climbing now
stood next to me at the light; she must know
every street here the way she maneuvered
the stroller over the curb. So she must know
who works up there, who files her papers in the cabinet
then leads her to the steel table.
One time when
my ovaries like stones were heavy with the chemistry
that multiplied millicell by cell every hour
I laid my body down
and a woman whose face was stone
held my hand. I think she hated her job
but knew how I felt.
I turn the corner
and sudden marigolds
heat the traffic island, another version
of garden, where men and women make their crossings
amid globes of orange fire. The workers seem to float into this morning
while I press my wish for the climbing woman,
that the face she sees

be vacant and spacious. That it leads her
the way sidewalks can,
solid, shaped to her feet
like sandals
worn thin, and smooth.

The Night Trains

I stood and watched the destruction of the Arcade,
a poor woman's *Milano* where ladies bought hats
and fancy boxes to keep them in. Then the tearing down
of the houses along the rivers,
whole neighborhoods slid under earth
where barrels and trunks from the old
countries rot inside the clay. We are trying to make

the haul-away go more quickly now, take the husks
and boxes of pipe, tubing, bodies of furnaces, warehouses
of loose rust and load them. We are trying to bury
all of it, we are trying to do what the old *studdabubbas*
hissed at us to do: Clean up after yourself before
someone else has to. But there's so much
mold and rust, I want to forget, late at night
in the minutes I try to save for rest

until I hear the trains coming through
carrying their garbage from New Jersey,
cars full of gauze and blood and human hair, teeth
and dull fur of the test animals.
How much have you lost?
Have you listened in happiness for a train
near your hour of sleep, listened for its generous
throat to fill the city air
with its burnt sugar and smoke? I
hear too many trains
after the 1:30 and before the 6.

I think about some lonely giant woman
having to clean up all the mess, she has to shovel
it into something, scrape everything into a bucket
tipped on its side, while sludge and girders roll
out again. She fills and fills her bucket, scrapes
the railyards and asphalt to ebony.
Still there is plenty
for the halls of the underground
city and its hurtful shine.

We Built This City

on violins and accordions,
eighteen-wheelers
and the Firing Squad of Henry Clay Frick.
Blood-stained panties
buried in landfills,
sweet and harmless drunks, too many to count.
The ideas if not the realities
of Pericles.
Coal buckets, work buckets, stolen goods.
Children dead because they were children.
Lost women.
Cocktail napkins covered with hieroglyphic
laments and secrets of the Universe.
Powdered human bonemass in vials
locked inside the biotechnology labs.
Cock rock, dyke rock,
proto-grunge and funk.
Jazz. Too many evolutions to count.
A stolen Picasso lithograph
bearing lyrics composed millennia ago.
Sleeping bags and Coleman lanterns.
Dogs, too many to count,
tongues congealed in 90-degree heat.
Veils on veils of strontium and benzene.
Christmas shoppers wading through snowdrifts,
     Smithfield Street, 10 p.m.
tunnel light, color of limestone.
Ingots, too many to count.
The *idea* of the Left Bank.

The idea of city.
Windows, 6 p.m., sunstruck, gray mabé pearls.
Timberlands, Wolverines, Sears Steeltoes
          balancing on scaffolding and airspace.
Rented tuxes, colors too many to name. Pussies wet and wet.
Kohl sticks worn down to nubs.
Application of the theory Marco Polo used to change Venice:
              Bring in news from the Outside.
Sidewalk gardens of eggplants and basil.
Flutes.
Tunnels like flutes.
The last of the Section Eight Urban Redevelopment Money.
The last of the UDAG Grants.
The last of the Nelson Rockefeller Republicans.
The Democratic Machine that ruled a century.
The idea of city.
The dream
     of what *polis* might mean.
The giant fusilli and ziti
of sewer pipes, too many to count.
The significance of the IRON OVER WATER
                          hexagram of the *I Ching*.
Office desks polished with lemon oil.
Rice cakes, rice paper, thin mats and bells.
A bridge half-woman, half-dragonfly.
Sharpened yellow pencils and fragrant gray lead.
Jaroslav Seifert's "Song of the Sweepings."

Eating Reagan

I got it
late, after the Oklahoma City bombing,
while counting the dots
on the *Wall Street Journal* map
marking Klan*Klan*Skinhead*Skinhead
outposts all over
my home state Pennsylvania
right above the Mason-Dixon Line
where the dots have been
all my life, down
past Uniontown and
the Maple Sugar Festival
in Meyersdale, down
near Old Route 40
where the deep mallow flowers
line the bike trail you can ride
all the way to D.C.
to Jefferson's cloud-white marble.

Once, when I woke to my first
schoolyear, when I watched
the black, white, and red America
and he came on selling soap
and his own Death Valley face,
I was excited with our new TV
and first pair of eyeglasses,
paying such close attention—
to a salesman who would be President
and I remember the handmade models

my fifth-grade class was so proud of—
Capitol, Parthenon, the old
Greek oath we memorized:
To be good citizens
"together with the help of all, or,
if not, single-handed."

Later, in a school I visited in the Eighties,
State Troopers were called out
to round up, to bring in,
and to end, once and for all,
the annual rite of cutting classes
on Senior Recognition Day:
the evil almost-grads
were marched back into the assembly room
and up onto the stage
before the sweating principal,
and the younger kids were marched in
past the gray guns and leather chinstraps
and seated, alphabetically,
to witness the example.

Kids wrote a letter
about their school food.
Ketchup was a vegetable,
hotdogs were entrees,
lunch tables were checkpoints.
They started showing me around:
sex was contraband you could get
behind the maintenance building.
A baby could be like a trophy
or a *fuck you*—if you had one
during senior year.

They were pretty good cynics.
A few were natural writers.

On the playground making poems
and drawings, we were so tiny
gazing up at the sky
and back toward the main entrance.
I told myself the world would be ours
because of *who we were*. I forgot
we make the republic
a few images and deeds at a time.
And nobody
including me
told those kids
their President was wrong.

Counting the dots I realized
Nixon was a dot.
Reagan was a dot.
I had eaten Reagan
like a dot
of blotter acid,
he was tough, pickled and shriveled,
the brain scar tissue and
media blockout
made him grainy
like old beef jerky.
Like one of the dolls from carny nights
when we were children,
the shrunken witch-heads we wasted quarters on
to try and win to scare our friends.
I swallowed him,
I absorbed him.
How were we to know he'd fool us?
He felt like nothing going down.

Star Gazing with My Brothers

I have to walk down through the cellar then up
through the little greenhouse
our father built instead of a bomb shelter in 1960—
I step out onto the patio where they're taking turns at the big scope,
and another of Jupiter's moons glides out from behind that gigantic
planet of emotions. Rege says we're standing under The Summer Triangle:
there's Albireo, the Double Star. The colors—how can clear fire have color?—
drug me, my father is on his chair murmuring the War in the Pacific
again: "The Equator was one big centrifugal force, coconuts were falling,
trees were swaying, Manos Island was the most beautiful place
but everyone was lonely." He laughs. Stars are in motion around
his body. I have to turn my back on him to look
into the tunnel that leads upward. Saturn's rings slant,
oily dust, here comes the white crystal of one of Jupiter's 79 moons.
Out here the zinnias touch my right shoulder. This one is black velvet,
this afternoon it was dark red, and these gray-white ones are pink
in daylight. My gray sandals are gray, my mother's voice is silver
falling down from the kitchen window
where she's wrapping food in foil for her shut-in neighbors
and she's delirious to have all her children here.
I ask Bob where Cassiopeia is and Rege answers. His son Paul
calls me over to get a look at M2 awash with studded
veils of stars on stars. He is so shy and beautiful I want to dance.
Now my brothers are assuring me
there is life as we know it in all the distant places.
Our mother the genius eavesdropper calls down, "Of course,
remember Copernicus."
Here is one of the centers of my world, so momentary
I wonder if it's even a system. A sister might mean anything

to her dreamers-for-brothers. I wish for *friend for life*. How easy
that feels, how fragile here at our childhood home
where every fir tree in the yard was once a tiny Christmas tree,
where the oldest dog is buried,
where I stand with my brothers, we have always been three.

The Ecology of Baseball

I personally know
at least three women who can throw the fastball.
Everybody knows
good women runners
and 20/20 vision outfielders.
Believe me,
I know women who can hit.

Live on cable,
thrilled insider her first triple
against a male pitcher,
the rookie picked herself up after the slide,
forgot herself
and hugged the third base coach.
"That kind of friendly shit has to go," one reporter, off-camera, said.
And the chattering—"It takes them fifteen minutes to finish
congratulating each other in the outfield," their coach complained.
But he sounded happy: "Women want it more
than men, they want to get up and start playing
early in the morning and just keep playing."

The past is alive here in the dirt
under square glass boxes at the feet of Clemente.
Our public relic
is the dirt he played on
behind the color barrier
he looked and laughed at.

Children pause to be photographed
beneath his hands
and hang onto his outstretched fingers.

The summer of the Last Big Strike
we took the (scab) replacements,
we wanted to fan ourselves
with playbooks sweet with new ink.
Hope for our city rested
on a 47-mile-per-hour knuckleball
or, ideally,

extra innings and long night games
where the women dress
in bright lipstick and flowered skirts
and the men chill out
and stuff their kids
with the healthy junk food.
And where lovers like the game to last,
a good slow kiss
slow enough to slow
our hard-working lives down.

Afterward when we file out,
sky black and silver with stars,
we out-swarm the traffic of insects
thickening around banks of lights.
Web of life, web of death,
now the hungry
nighthawks glide in to feast.
All theirs, the shiny bowl and crusted seats.
They swerve into every concentric aisle of air,
driven into it, the cleaning, the sweep.

Tell Me about the Peacocks and Fountains

I put the Dante away, the poem
was beautiful but the critic's
intrusion on the text made me dizzy.
I had to see him:
the one in the tight chinos
had to see his drum set
his double martini glasses
his bar with the translucent lights
had to see him
turning down his sheets
me in them
had to see his neon condoms
him sliding one on
so I reached for the street
the curb the car door and took the back streets
where tiny houses were so lit up:
I was driving down an aisle
wet as black enamel
up his sidewalk to his door
and goldfish in their shallow china bowl
like Mary McCarthy's fish in Venice
(they were languid but alive)
He was brooding but drew me to him
leg slung over a wide red chair
pulled me onto his lap
and I was widening
into his open shirt
He told me again
Here we are among the peacocks and fountains

Small cats watched from their intaglio pillows
It was years ago in the poise
of his lightly tanned shoulders
and my dark rose tunic
and how he unfastened it
when I asked him to

Night Walks

Tonight I feel like a lucky coin
far from the fields where no one walks:
East of the city I open my eyes, Tu Fu said.
Out there where the edge of the city thins away
sumac and locust call to me
to walk off into folds of snow
hemming the tree trunks
      where horses stand near graves—
                   my oldest dead—

Out there the willows
whose branches are thin as Roma whips
rasp the old town's name: Rzeszow, beloved Carpathian town
of the old little mothers:

Like a whip
my mother's name: Gunia/horsehair.
Edge of the village square
one *gestapo* follows my mother's mother
who has stepped out of her kitchen
to smoke a cigar, then stand in line for bread.
He eyes her like a camera
        though no pictures of that time
were made.

Out here my mind clears, my body emerges
to take the shape of space
the walk gives it.
   Wary, I'm in awe of the blue roads, here,

at the edge of my city
winding me back in.
Flanks of our ancient hills
wear hundreds of shades of brown and gray.
Roads coil and uncoil
over our wide basins,
our waterways and inlets,
channels now feeble, now flooded.
Brooklets and gutters run hard
after this morning's heavy summer storm.
The form of a city changes faster than the heart of a mortal.

Melancholy's like reading Rilke:
being slowly and sweetly poisoned to death,
                              death by IV from the stars,
by way of the sky's open vault.
Moody night, you have something to do
                    with rage,
with houselessness,
        though I have a house
tight as a ship
and with as many leaks and hiding places.
I gave up on Rilke when I decided I'm still not old enough
to read him. I walk.
        Up the avenues and through parking lots
and bus stops where it gets hazy and backlit after twelve.

        There's only one human that I know of
sleeping on cardboard near the Carnegie.
The vents are broad there
and the foyers of the University
are generously dark.
I'm taking the side streets now,
        I'm under lights
and can be seen and safe.

Down by the rivers there are more
sleeping under bridges, sleeping against the bulwarks.

There is no consciousness anymore except in the streets
because there is history only in the streets,
so runs the decree, Camus said.
            He was sad, hungry for the sea,
evening meditations.
        All my teachers
have given me the same gift:
writing is a walk,
never the same twice.
        Someone from the city paper
tried living under the bridges and reporting about it
but he was attacked
in print
    because he could go home to his apartment
every night if he wanted to, after all.
That is privilege.

But I say make use of it.
If you can't sleep, get up.

from *Level Green*

(1990)

Moving to New York

—for G.M.

When you get there, walk into the Café Deutschland,
not the painting by Jörg Immendorf, but a bar I'm imagining
and the cold will leave you like a jacket dropped to the floor
before a blazing fire, orange ceiling, blue walls,
a green leather floor still warm from the women
getting up to leave (not on your account; they're off
to another party). Order a drink, hot and strong; everyone looks
ready, their clean hair and thick sweaters breathing at you,
the paintings are amazing: a country scene folds in on itself
forever, its tiny scale happy and intricate, like you.

The night you left
you joined a long list of expatriates,
all my old friends gone to California
or East. Industry was dead ten years ago
and our country of two classes, one called *retrain*,
the other *acquire*, moves on, wobbly and mean.
You stretch into a future, funneling canvases in
from Germany (another country in need of a culture).
The young Expressionists want to meet you.
They have. They're happy they're painting and making
money and small businesses and talking about
where they buy their jeans. And they make good art!
About your one worry—you'll survive as an organism
in the big streets and small greeneries.
The morning coffee tastes good as you ride
up the elevator, and when you ride down at night

149

the steel doors open, the great glass doors
of the building hush closed, and you walk into
the avenue, the city silver and black
as your eyeglasses and coat.

Fabian

was to Elvis
as Travolta is to Springsteen
is to
Rock itself,
and my brothers said
he was gay,

but I forgot I was sixteen and too old to care
one night in a pizzeria in Montclair, 1967.
I was in love with the boys
at the counter
whose wet black hair
curled over their white shirt collars. They handled
the slender bottles of olive oil,
talked on the phone, joked and sang
to each other in Sicilian
thick and bronze as their fingers and lips.
I practiced a dangerous
and hopeless look
and stepped up to the counter
of the True Italy, far from Pittsburgh
and its ignorance of classic lust
and I wanted those boys

as much as I wanted Fabian
and his voice on the box and I was
on top of him, pretty greaser,
his hands grabbing me around the waist
tossing me into the air high above

the tight olives and pepperoni discs
sweating in their steel bins and I
flew, with Fabian, the palms of our hands
sticky with flour and spice.

Father's Magic Trick

He could grab the hot casserole and dance
the kitchen with it while we clapped
and squealed at him never to put it down.
"I have hot hands," he'd sing and laugh
at supper when I pretended I was the meteor girl

who stood beside him leaning over the pool
inside the nuclear dome where he worked
adjusting fuel rods like pickup sticks
to stoke the fire that meant
heat, light, wealth for us all.

He worked with his hands tying
fuel bundles in the chambers of Fermi and Chalk River.
His hands were thick as oven mitts,
safe enough after touching the atomic fire
to touch anything. Down in the cellar
welding toys and lawn chairs bare-handed
he always had an audience at the window,
kids peering in at the strobes
watching him bend over his
blue flame and wand.

The Nuclear Accident at SL 1, Idaho Falls, 1961

My father remembers a nurse
talking from her hospital bed,
off-limits in her dome, like a ghost
or captured angel, still full of what
she'd managed to do: climb the ladder,
free the man so hot they had to wait
before burying him, till they scraped
his skin and cleaned his bones.
After three weeks she was still alive
and slowly dying, telling the
ridiculous bad luck of it:

A guy's standing, settling the fuel bundle
into the reactor
and his buddy comes up and gooses him.
The bundle jerks, the lid of the great
vessel slides open and off. The guy
is blasted up
impaled to the ceiling
by a shaft of steam and a metal rod,
his white-suited body
stuck up there
and no one,
all of them evacuated,
can get him down till
days later the medical team
enters the containment
in jumpsuits and booties.

My father remembers the nurse
entering the dome, pretty and bright.

It takes brilliance to be a heroine
and something secret and stupid.
She walks across the gleaming floor,
places her foot on the first rung
then the next, climbs up.
She must know how stupid this is.
It's only a body up there
and the air is invisible
with what will kill her.
Has anyone given her anything to take along
on this trip? Rabbit foot? Heart on a chain?
Can she see anything in the face looking
down at her? She holds herself
up. She pulls him down.
She walks to the ambulance and lead coffin.
She knows what she is doing.
She knows what she has to do.

Looking for Level Green

Seneca told a white man
the way to Fort Duquesne
was "West. Two days through forest.
Then cross a long, level green."

Now a suburb of the suburb of
Monroeville, home of the nondestructive
Nuclear Facility. No uranium on site.
No plutonium. No more blue collars.

Ten minutes, though, and you're in a green
pocket called Daugherty's Grove
where my parents fell in love
where bluebells drift behind gas pumps
standing sentinel to a sad forest of dwarves.

Ten minutes from the fat cool mall and condos
framing the thruway
stands Roundtop, old burial mound, ignoring
anyone's wishes to dig bones or potsherds or memories.
A girl can lie down there and not think, for once.

And ten minutes from the weapons site
that has no dripping, leaking
or raw oily places
slouches the Shades of Death

where a woman killed herself for love.
There's nothing but
tall pines down in there
alive and holy, alive with her.

Fourteen Nights

The radiator clanks its February chimes
and I'm awake all night with fresh coffee and headphones
feeding me Italian, the one constant aphrodisiac:
Ecco un'arancia/here's an orange
and I make my way back to Lodi via the night train
and the weekend sailors came aboard carrying
baskets of fruit, salami and olives, sharing
all with me and I first understood all soldiers
are boys pledged to death. They kissed me and waved
when I got off near my flat above the butcher shop
where sparrows hung by their ankles
and I walked the twenty iron steps up
to my unheated rooms. Above the piazza
whose Romanesque arches were my bookends
I read all of Lawrence and watched
the Italian presidential elections on TV
fourteen nights straight.
Letters from home that winter
with their all-night sex and refined organic mescaline
made me sick for love.
I sat under the bronze lamp and red blanket
reading the novels and when Birkin ran
into the forest, scraping himself on branches
and rocks, I wanted to look into the faces
of all the men I'd never slept with
but thought about and ask
why he did that. The men I knew then
would have said it was his *masculine soul*
uniting with Nature, green and powerful enough

to annihilate everything. Death and joy riveted
Lawrence, but so did unhappy sex, bottled up
and inspected. I figured the Italians
knew better with their shouting and cigars.
They loved the secret ballot and clean white paper.
They loved deep coffee and microphones and endless
voting because it meant endless choosing.

At the end of loneliness
I discovered the good poems
and their impossible burn.
I read them on trains passing
the small Autostrada towns, Biella
and Santhia reminding me of all the
Pittsburgh towns bloodless Mencken missed
on his train ride through
"the libido for the ugly."
The mafiosi villages where my uncles
knew which bars gave credit and which
opened to the secret knock.
I thought I was different from everyone then,
a woman alone on a train
loneliest woman in the world
burning to make my choices.

Sheila's Flat

Stencils everywhere: ducks, trees, demitasse
cups, a window she knocked out with a sledgehammer,
smaller and larger versions of that window stenciled
on every available foot of ceiling and loft

and a giant hookah with mouthpieces that look
like nipples, though all the girls tell her it's
politically incorrect to call them that

and in the kitchen Sheila is heating milk
and working on a new canvas and video
simultaneously and I am in the bathroom checking
her latest reading material including the *Greenfield
Green Tab* and *Gemology Journal* and her preserved copy

of our manifesto that demanded tampax—
Free to All People—at every Turnpike
entrance and exit, and I am looking
out her window onto the South Side

and her garden which after rain
radiates out like a map of Paris
but whose beds are named

Silvermound Artemesia
Violet Way
Avenue of the Lobelia

My Grandmother's Rags

My Baci watched for Louie the huckster
and potato sacks he saved for her,
wrappings for boxes sent to the town I couldn't
pronounce, Rzeszow, east of Krakow.
The work took all day,
sewing rags around the box edges,
then the sewing of the name.
Baci's fine spidery hand
moved across the address square
fifteen stitches per inch.

My grandmother came from the old country
and sent back dresses with plastic belts,
delicate rayon scarves, packets of coffee
and Camels tucked into white shoes.
For herself she saved the paper from bread,
jar lids and rubber bands. Her daily work
began with rags. Menstrual rags for her
daughters even after bleaching bore sepia
clouds, and clouds of steam lifted as she pressed
rags for the bed for whatever she coughed up
during the night.

She loved anything paisley,
and cheesecake from Rhea's Bakery, and the tissue
around the cake which she kept beside clove
and cinnamon and the good rags.
I saw her use only one,

the lace handkerchief
on weddings and the hot, bad days,
wrapped around a potato, arthritis medicine,
for its fresh magic.

Smoking Cigars with Li Po

There must be a way I can lose everything by throwing myself
on the floor and untying my kimono, or, better, having it untied

by one of your dancing girls—where are they? I remember the one
with dark hair who kissed me and said, "You're always kvetching

about something and you don't even know what you want," and I didn't but
I'm burning faster than ever, I'm writing the poem, I tilt

my eyebrows to the angle of the room and squint you to the typewriter
voluptuous and blunt as grappa. You unwrap two Garcia y Vegas, teach me:

the secret of the inhale is to forget all since adolescence.
You say, "I didn't know *that*!" when I tell you about Che and

Beauvoir. You speak Turkish and Jamaican and pure talk I haven't
heard much since 1969. I'm learning photographic memory.

I already know the patience of the Iron Goddess, at least
I think I do since I'm in love with at least two dreams at a time

and I don't believe in coded language, I want to wander like you,
crazy uncle, home on my back. I don't believe in, say, Gertrude

Stein's baby sleeping in white eyelet in her perfect garden. I only
see Alice emptying the diaper pail again. I'm more interested in

Amy Lowell's cigars and the penis for its own sake—and time
give me time hot hot as the match I strike now and raise to my lips.

Why you, Li Po, so far and so close? Whatever it is we might have in common
is our crookedness, you, bent over a waterfall, singing, and me,

leaning over Turtle Creek, looking for crayfish, looking for my
Level Green, which was not level but was so green I thought

Earth dropped off at the crest of my hill where the trees
waved like plumes against the cobalt universe. If it's true

that you went out while trying to grasp the moon
I'll hang the full moon of my childhood over you,

I'll stand up and keep on taking the test
I'll wash this floor only to dance on it
night and day long,
my hair going up in smoke.

Acknowledgments

I am grateful to the editors of the following journals, in which some of the new poems have appeared or are about to appear, often in different versions or under different titles:

Barrow Street—"Young Jane Jacobs"

Epiphany: The Borders Issue—"An Elixir of Mica"

Italian Americana—"Doppelgänger" (as "The Strange Building"), "The Immolation," "Open, Grove"

Plume—"To a New Window"

The Poetry Distillery @poetrybarn.org (an e-chapbook)—"The Reader"

Southern Indiana Review—"Pittsburgh Maps"

I remain grateful to the editors of these presses and journals, and to the editors who reprinted poems in anthologies:

The Apollonia Poems (University of Wisconsin Press, 2017; Four Lakes Prize)

The Water Books (Autumn House Press, 2012)

Reactor (University of Wisconsin Press, 2004)

The Door Open to the Fire (Cleveland State University Press, 1997)

Level Green (University of Wisconsin Press, 1991; Brittingham Prize)

Black Butterfly (Center for Book Arts Prize, 1997; limited edition)

Agni, Along These Rivers: Poetry and Photography from Pittsburgh, Astarte, Border Lines: Poems of Migration, Connotation Press, Crab Orchard Review, The Great River Review, The Illinois Review, Laurel Review, Library Reading Series, Living Inland, Many Mountains Moving, the minnesota review, New South, Pearl, Pittsburgh Poetry Review, Poetry International, Prairie Schooner, The Stillwater Review, West Branch, Witness, The Women's Review of Books.

Special thanks to Ted Lardner (Cleveland State University Press), Michael Sims (Autumn House), and Sharon Dolin (Center for Book Arts). Thanks are also due to the Corporation of Yaddo and the American Academy in Rome for residency fellowships, for quiet and nourishment.

Many people have read and commented on my work over the years. For their close reading and patience, and for their support of my work in myriad ways, I thank Patricia Dobler and Peter Oresick. I thank Ed Ochester, Gerald Stern, Mary Oliver, Michael S. Harper, Alicia Ostriker, Afaa Michael Weaver, Liz Rosenberg, Mary Taylor Simeti, Maggie Anderson, Lynn Emanuel, Anne Waldman, Anne Marie Macari, Mara Scanlon, Norman Scanlon, Shannon Sankey, Timothy Gebadlo, Lynne McEniry, and Marisa Frasca. Salutes and thanks to The Real Wildsisters, Alexander Olawaiye, Cathy Jackson, Katherine Steinmetz, Rosanne Berubé, Marie Sauret, Sean Beckford, Louise Silk, Stephanie Flom, and Frances Baker.

Warmest to Geeta Kothari, Toi Derricotte, and Jan Beatty, with gratitude for your work, and for mini-retreats, library sessions, and razor-sharp consultations.

Finally, my deep gratitude to Adam Mehring and the staff at the University of Wisconsin Press. Thank you Sean Bishop, Jesse Lee Kercheval, and, most of all, Ron Wallace, for support over many years.

Notes

New Poems

"Young Jane Jacobs"—Information about both the formal and informal education of American-Canadian urbanist Jane Jacobs (1916–2006) is detailed in *Eyes on the Street: The Life of Jane Jacobs* by Robert Kanigel (Vintage, 2017). The poem references Kanigel's account of Jacobs's dislike of primary school.

"A Visit from Milosz"—The poem includes variations on a few phrases from *Conversations with Czeslaw Milosz* by Ewa Czarnecka and Aleksander Fiut (Harcourt Brace Jovanovich, 1987). *Laskawa melancholia* can be translated as "kind" or "gracious melancholy."

"Young George Harrison"—Enormous thanks to Don Hollowood for sharing his knowledge about Harrison's technical sound craft.

"The Diagonals"— The poem includes my variation on lines 14 and 15 from *Inferno XXV* in Dante's *Divine Comedy*.

"The Sound Boat"—The tailor is at work near Via Dondalo in Trastevere, Rome.

The Apollonia Poems

"Mother Comes"—*Kto wie* means "Who knows?"

Reactor

"In Praise of Camus at the End of His Century"—The italicized phrases and sentences are from Albert Camus' *American Journals* (Marlowe & Company, 1995).

The Door Open to the Fire

"Night Walks"—*The form of a city changes faster than the heart of a mortal* is my variation of lines found in Charles Baudelaire's poem "The Swan." *There is no consciousness anymore except in the streets because there is history only in the streets, so runs the decree* is from Albert Camus' American Journals (Marlowe and Company, 1995).

WISCONSIN POETRY SERIES

Edited by Ronald Wallace and Sean Bishop

(B) = Winner of the Brittingham Prize in Poetry

(FP) = Winner of the Felix Pollak Prize in Poetry

(4L) = Winner of the Four Lakes Prize in Poetry